A Gift For

Lisa

From

Kristi

## *Joys of* FRIENDSHIP
### A Celebration *of* Girlfriends

Copyright © 2004 Hallmark Licensing, Inc.

Published by Hallmark Books, a division of Hallmark Cards, Inc.,
Kansas City, MO 64141
Visit us on the Web at www.Hallmark.com.

Editorial Development: Olivia Cytrynowicz
Designed by: Walé Adeniran
Art Director: Mark Cordes

Inspired by the thoughts and writings of: Suzanne Berry, Bill Bridgeman, Keely Chace, Chris Conti, Chris Brethwaite, Olivia Cytrynowicz, Renée Duvall, Jennifer Fujita, Matt Gowen, Cheryl Hawkinson, Suzanne Heins, Dee Ann Stewart, Bill Gray, Carolyn Hoppe, Jim Howard, Allyson Jones, Barbara Loots, Laurie Monsees, Mark Oatman, John Peterson, Dan Taylor, Alarie Tennille, Dean Walley, Molly Wigand

Printed and bound in China
BOK4089

GIFT BOOKS
*from Hallmark*

# *Joys* of FRIENDSHIP

## A Celebration *of* Girlfriends

*Friendship is...*

…a gift

that can be opened every day,

and it still holds

lots of *happy*, sweet surprises.


This warm-hearted and witty collection

celebrates the ordinary, everyday moments

that make our friendships so extraordinary.

From *laughing* together

to going on (and off) diets together,

good friends always bring out

the best in each other.

*Friendship is
a smiley
kind of feeling.*

*Have friends*, will giggle.

*Girlfriends* help you

make nonsense of the world.

The *visit's* always too short

when the *company's fun*.

ALL THE PLACES, ALL THE FUD - RACES,
PARTIES, HHI, DI, MARCO & ALL
THE MORE TO COME !!
OMG - IS THIS US OR WHAT ?!?

How can you ever be done talking

with such a *good friend?*

... 361.58 MINS. LATER & 1:30AM—HAVE
TO HANG UP OUT OF NECESSITY!!

*It's the friends* we meet along life's way
who make the trip more fun.

. . . Who You TELL'IN ?!

*A friend* is quick
to listen, slow to
judge, and always
ready to shop. ☺

*Friends* are always
having way more fun
than it really makes *sense*
to be having.

ALWAYS!!

When the *laughter is light*

and the memories are many

but the time is too short...

you know you're with

a *friend.*

... So MANY GREAT MEMORIES!

*Laughing* when
they shouldn't be laughing
is some of the best laughing
*friends do.*

OOPS! ALL THOSE
"INSIDE" JOKES!! ("CC")

*A friend* can

make you smile —

even when *she's* not around.

AGAIN, ALL THOSE INSIDE JOKES...
LITTLE PRETTY KITTY!

*A good friend...*

...knows to call in between

your favorite shows.

*A good friend...*

...has your *kids'* birthdays

marked on her calendar.

Duh ?! (2/6)
(2/8)

*A good friend...*

...shares *ideas, dreams,*
and the makeup counter gift
with purchase.

*A good friend…*

…knows what kind
of *ice cream* to bring you
when you're *sick.*

*A good friend...*

... will go to a movie with you—

even if she's already seen it.

THIS IS A LO-BRAINER! HOW
MANY TIMES HAVE WE SAID... "I'LL
GO SEE IT W/ YOU AGAIN!"

*A good friend...*

...pretends not to notice
the litter box smell.

YEAH, BECAUSE WE WOULDN'T
HAVE ONE!

*A good friend...*

...can *always* find something good
to say about your bad haircut.

HILLARIOUS!!

*A good friend...*

...will quietly *destroy*
the photograph that makes you
look like a *beached* whale.

LOVED THIS!

*A good friend...*

...will also destroy
the negative of the photograph
that makes you look like
a *beached whale.*

*A good friend…*

…will go on the *same diet*

with you—and off it, too.

"FATTIES"!!

...calls just to say "*hi.*"

... OR DOESN'T, BUT YOU KNOW
SHE'S THINKING IT!

*A good friend...*

...calls back if you don't

sound quite like *yourself.*

# Friendship is...

...laughing at the same things.

... one dessert and two forks.

...really being *understood*.

...never running out of things to talk about.

...*borrowing* each other's clothes.

... knowing someone by heart.

...being accepted *unconditionally*.

... having someone to cheer you on.

...*picking up* right where you left off.

... there when you need it.

... *Always*

A friend knows
everything
about you
and loves you
anyway.

*A friend* is the one
who holds the mirror
so you can see yourself
more clearly.

*Friends* finish

each other's sentences,

know what the other is thinking...

oh, and they eat

way too much ~~chocolate~~.

''' (OF EVERYTHING ELSE!)

The better *the friend,*

the less cleaning

you do before

she comes over.

AMEN, SISTA' !!

*Friends* can make you laugh
like no one *else* can.

OMG!! THINK OF ALL THE
"SILLY" THINGS...

Between *friends,*

words are *optional.*

A friend can tell

how your day has been

by the way you say

*"Hello."*

YES,
ALWAYS!

*A friend* is someone
who keeps your secrets,
laughs at your jokes,
and can always tell
the *difference*.

IT'S FUNNY TO ME!

*When you're in a bad mood, your friend . . .*

… isn't overly *cheerful*.

… brings you a plant from the supermarket.

… agrees with whatever you say.

… will sacrifice *sleep* on a weeknight to talk about it.

… brings tissues.

… feeds you something with calories…

many, many calories.

… makes you *smile* (no matter how long it takes).

… forgives you ahead of time for all the bad moody

stuff you'll probably say.

… will track down whoever's responsible and drown

the guilty party in *guilt* and *insults*.

… gently reminds you that things aren't that bad.

*Friends make the good things better and the bad things not so bad... simply by being there.*

Because the sun
can't shine every day,
we have good
*friends.*

One of
the secrets of *life*
is keeping your friends
within hugging
distance.

The *best* cure for a bad day
is a good *friend*.

It's so very relaxing,
completely untaxing
to let loose and unwind
with good *friends*.

*Friendship—*

Good for the soul
but lousy for the diet.

Burs it's fun!!
"ATHENA"

*Friends* are the best kind of therapy.

There's no problem *friends* can't solve
with enough time and chocolate.

*Things you can tell a friend . . .*

- "Sometimes bad perms happen to good people."

- Your real weight.

- The *worst* thing you've ever done.

- That you really bought it premade at the supermarket.

- That she has *lipstick* on her teeth.

- About your hot flashes and night sweats.

- "I just ate an entire bag of potato chips."

- Things you wouldn't tell your *mother*.

- About all your boyfriend's/husband's annoying habits.

- That you *cry* at soup commercials. (I DON'T KNOW WHAT THEY'RE TALKING ABOUT.)

YES, YES, YES...!

*Friends always see the best in each other.*

*A friend* still laughs
even when you've told a joke
completely wrong.

*A friend* celebrates
the goodness and greatness
that is *uniquely* you.

✗ HERE WE ARE!! FAST-
FORWARD... DI 2030!!

*Good friends* don't mind

when you sing along with the car radio.

✱ MARCO IS., FL. / MAY 2006
CONVERTIBLE PT CRUISER
AIN'T LIFE GRAND!!

*Friends* are the family
we didn't start out with
who make us *feel* likable,
funny, and clever.

*. . .* BETTER THAN FAMILY, EVEN!!

Chase away the blues,

laugh away the time...

it's safe– *a friend* is here.

*A smile* from a friend says,

"You are *welcome* here."

The
very *best friends*
have the kind
of relationship where each
thinks *she's* getting
the better part
of the deal.

*A friend*
always has a warm
and wonderful way
of making you feel
*loved.*

Hallmark would love to hear from you.

Please send your comments to:

Book Feedback

Hallmark Cards, Inc.

2501 McGee, Mail Drop 250

Kansas City, MO  64141-6580.

Or e-mail us at

booknotes@Hallmark.com.